TIDES *of* CHANGE

In memory of my father,
who taught me passion and persistence,
and forgave my lack of patience.
S.M.

To my mom, Elsie,
for always encouraging me
and
in memory of my dad, Ken, who taught me
where to look to find nature
and how to see so that I might enjoy it.
K.C.

TIDES *of* CHANGE

Faces of the Northwest Coast

SHERYL McFARLANE & KEN CAMPBELL

Do you know the Northwest Coast? Do you know her many histories?

Petroglyphs carved into stone by ancient peoples are doorways to ten thousand years of past.

Ship logs and charts reveal exploration routes. But do they tell of the hopes and fears of sailors who sought gold and furs and a fabled sea-link to the Orient?

Its hard to imagine that the name on this weathered gravestone once belonged to a child who skipped and sang and played as you do now.

Solitary lighthouse keepers have signalled the dangers of coastal waterways for more than a century. And when the fog rolls in so thick it's like a wall, passing ships are still thankful for the blast of invisible foghorns.

The rough and ready lumberjacks of yesterday measured giant Sitka Spruce and Douglas Fir in board feet and the time it took to fall them with sweat and two-man saws.

When you peer through the sagging doorways of a deserted coastal town, can you hear the cry of "GOLD," or was that just the wind whistling through the trees?

Have you seen kayakers challenging the sea? This coast has sparked the spirit of adventure many times before. Names like Quadra, Cook, Bering and Vancouver ring out along northwest shores.

Do you know the Northwest Coast? Do you know her people?

Have you met artists carving windows into their culture with every new totem pole they raise?

On chilly winter mornings before first light has touched the bay, the lowest yearly tides announce the beginning of the clam diggers' day.

Do you know rubber-booted cannery workers, bone-weary when the sun is sinking low and one last fishboat is still unloading at the docks?

Have you seen the children of isolated shores and windswept islands waiting for the schoolboat in the early morning drizzle?

Or known the anxious families of a troller crew forced to wait out a sudden summer storm in a distant cove?

You've seen tugs towing ships a hundred times their size, but not the taut muscles of the skipper's jaw. Once safely through the churning narrows, he shares a grin with his daughter, a third-generation tug captain in the making.

Walk past downtown docks to Chinatown with its bustling market stalls, narrow streets and crowded shops. The dragons that twist and writhe on doorways, signs and kites recall ancient mythologies to life.

Do you know the Northwest Coast? Do you know the many faces of her beauty?

Have you walked along a beach wiped clean like an empty slate? Your footprints are as fleeting as the shifting dunes of sand rising in the distance.

Imagine water spraying skyscraper-high when a wall of ice breaks free and crashes into the ocean. The glacier's chill will make you shiver even on a twenty-hour summer day.

Have you watched a dozen sea lions at play in the frothy water or seen their frantic rush to reach the shore when a pod of transient orcas surfaces too near?

You could lose an afternoon exploring tidepool treasures, where fascinating worlds in miniature are daily nourished by the sea.

Climb the rocky bluffs to watch Grey Whales pass on one of the longest migrations of any mammal known. Whalers called them devilfish long ago. But those who reach out to touch their barnacle-encrusted skin know them now as the gentle giants.

Follow the banks of a river teeming with the struggles of spawning salmon. Have you ever wondered how they find their way from the open sea? Or how bald eagles seem to know exactly when to be there waiting for their yearly salmon feast?

Old growth coastal forests touched by a hundred thousand days of mist and rain have existed for an eternity. Yet we've only just begun to understand the intricacy of this living tapestry.

Do you know the Northwest Coast?

Have you seen the tides of change that have swept her shores and touched her people?

Will you shape her future, or will her winds and tides and waves shape yours?

Tidbits I discovered . . .

Radiocarbon dating is an important tool for estimating the age of very old objects. But, it's no help for dating petroglyphs since they contain no carbon. One petroglyph depicting a paddlewheel steamer must have been carved after 1836, the year the first paddle steamer arrived on the Northwest coast. A reliable means of dating petroglyphs has not yet been discovered. (page 5)

This **Nuu-chah-nulth** version of Captain Cook's first visit to Vancouver Island in 1778 is very different from the one most history books have recorded. Long ago the people of Yuquot were surprised by two strange ships. They welcomed the strangers by leading them to safety. The villagers cried, "Nu·tka·ʔičim," ("go around the point"). The strangers thought the villagers were introducing themselves as Nootka. The Nuu-chah-nulth people have been wrongly called Nootka Indians ever since. (page 6)

Today, a cough might keep you home from school for a few days. But before the introduction of antibiotics and immunizations, **whooping cough (pertussis)** was only one of many illnesses that caused the deaths of thousands of children each year. (page 7)

In 1906, **Minnie Patterson**, wife of the Cape Beale Lighthouse keeper, made headlines for her heroic, four hour ordeal to get help for the crew of a sinking ship during a storm. She was awarded a medal, but most keepers and their families remain unknown and unsung heroes. (page 8)

Before the days of chainsaws, some trees could take hand-loggers an entire day to take down. The remains of **springboards** can still sometimes be found embedded in tree stumps. These narrow platforms were used to raise the loggers above the butt-swell of the tree, reducing the amount of wood they had to cut through. (page 9)

In 1896, Skagua (now Skagway, Alaska) was an isolated Tlingit village. In two years, it grew to more than 20,000 people. At its peak, the town boasted 19 restaurants, 15 general stores, and 4 newspapers. A few years later, its population plunged to less than 500. Why? The **Klondike Gold Rush** had come and gone! (page 10)

Today, most kayaks are made from modern materials such as fibreglass or kevlar. But, their basic design has not changed from the **closed-skin boats** Aleutian whale hunters relied on for thousands of years. Aleutians even had their own version of waterproof jackets or **kamleikas**. These were made by carefully stitching together strips of sea lion or walrus intestines. (page 11)

Since the earliest carvers had no hard metals, the first **totem poles** were carved using blades made out of sharpened shells, stone or bone and often took many years to complete. (page 13)

Clams belong to a huge group of two-shelled animals called bivalves. Not all clams are harmless. **Toredos or shipworms** are very destructive wood-boring clams. The shells of these worm-like animals do not house them, but are modified raspers for tunnelling through wood. (page 14)

Today, most of us take canned food for granted. But, scientists believe that lead poisoning from canned food may have helped to doom the famous **Franklin Expedition** of 1845. The body of one crew member was exhumed and tested for lead poisoning in 1986. They found more than enough lead to have caused his death. (page 15)

Much of the Northwest coast is either too rugged or too isolated to be accessible by land. Instead of cars, people in these communities rely on boats to get around, including **school boats**! (page 16)

A fishboat is a fishboat is a fishboat. Right? Wrong! **Trollers** trail fish lines suspended from rigging, while **seiners** rely on a vertical net wall to trap their catch. Sheets of netting are dropped into the water with floats at the top and weights at bottom. Fish are scooped up by pulling the bottom of the net up and in. **Gillnetters** are a whole other story! (page 17)

The first tugs were really passenger and freighter steamships like the *Beaver*. They sometimes pulled a tow because they were the only power boats around. (page 18)

Chinese immigrants brought a rich and vastly different cultural heritage to their new homes on the Northwest Coast. Traditions like the Dragon Dance attract thousands. Unlike the feared, fire-breathing dragons of European folklore, Chinese **cloud-breathing dragons** are revered. They are associated with strength, renewal and good fortune. (page 19)

What is not alive but is constantly on the move? Sand dunes! Tough **dunegrass, sedge** and **beach pines** help to stabilize most coastal dunes. Dunegrass was also widely used by several Northwest coast tribes for a variety of woven articles. (page 21)

Have you ever wondered why glaciers seem to look blue? It all has to do with snow! It's probably no surprise that snow is 90% air. The other 10% is delicate, star-shaped crystals of frozen water vapour. The snow at the bottom of a glacier has had most of the air squeezed out from between these crystals, so it reflects mainly blue light. Scientists have given the name **blue ice** to this very dense glacial snow. Since icebergs break or **calve** off glaciers, they also contain blue ice. (page 22)

The Northwest coast is home to two types of orcas or killer whales. **Transients** and **residents** are different in almost every way. Residents are found in the same places at the same times, year after year. They live in large pods of up to fifty whales, and tend to rely mainly on a diet of fish. Transients travel alone or in small pods of less than six and feed primarily on marine mammals such as sea lions. Their migration patterns remain a mystery. (page 23)

Purple sea stars may be common, but some of their adaptations are most unusual! They can regrow lost arms—handy if you have a twenty-year lifespan. And it's a good thing they don't need shoes for their thousand-plus tube-like feet. Stranger still—their idea of dining out is to push their own stomach into their prey's shell where it digests its meal before returning home! (page 24)

Grey whales are infected with a unique **barnacle** larvae just after birth. Once attached to the whale's blubber, these freeloading filter feeders are guaranteed a constant food supply. They travel with the whales on an annual 15,000 to 18,000 kilometre migration from Baja, Mexico to the Bering or Chukchi Seas and back again. It will be the only home these barnacles will ever know, and if the whale dies, the barnacles die with it. (page 25)

One short stretch of the Chilkat River in Alaska has been known to attract as many as 3,495 **bald eagles** during salmon spawning season. But, in 1994, an astounding 3,766 bald eagles were recorded at a site on the Squamish River in British Columbia! (page 26)

Imagine a tree as tall as a thirty-storey building. Just such a tree—a 95-metre **Sitka spruce**—is the largest of its kind in the world. It can be found towering above its Carmanah Valley neighbours on Vancouver Island in British Columbia. (page 27)

Yet there's so much more . . .

Buried in Ice: The Mystery of A Lost Arctic Expedition, W. Beatie / J. Geiger (Scholastic/Maddison Press, 1992)

Carving A Totem Pole, Vickie Jensen (Douglas & McIntyre, 1994)

Eagles, Charlene Gieck (North Word Press Inc., 1991)

Exploring an Ocean Tide Pool, Jeanne Bendick (Henry Holt & Co. Inc., 1992)

Gray Whales, D. Gordon / A. Baldridge (Monterey Bay Aquarium, 1991)

Green Giants, Tom Parkin (Douglas & McIntyre, 1992)

Indian Rock Carvings of the Pacific Northwest Coast, Beth Hill (Hancock House Pub., 1975)

In the Company of Whales, Alexandra Morton (Orca Book Publishers Ltd., 1993)

The Klondike Stampede, Pierre Berton (McClelland & Stewart Inc., 1991)

Polar Passage, J. MacInnis (Ballantine Books, U.S. / Random House, Canada, 1989)

The Power of Ice, R. Radlauer / L. Gitkin (Children's Press, 1985)

Raincoast Chronicles: First Five, Howard White, editor (Harbour Publishing, 1976)

Tales from Gold Mountain: Stories of the Chinese in the New World, Paul Yee (Douglas & McIntyre, 1989)

Text copyright © 1995 Sheryl McFarlane
Illustration copyright © 1995 Ken Campbell

Canadian Cataloguing in Publication Data
McFarlane, Sheryl, 1954-
The tides of change

ISBN 1-55143-040-1 (bound)
I. Pacific Coast (B.C.) — Juvenile literature   I. Campbell, Ken, 1950-   II. Title.
FC3845.P2M33 1995   j971.1'1   C95-910452-6   F1089.P2M33 1995

Publication assistance provided by The Canada Council.

Design by Ken Campbell
Printed and bound in Hong Kong

Orca Book Publishers Ltd.
P.O. Box 5626, Station B
Victoria, BC Canada
V8R 6S4

Orca Book Publishers Ltd.
P.O. Box 468
Custer, WA   USA
98240-0468

10   9   8   7   6   5   4   3   2   1